WINNING
BLACKJACK

WITHOUT COUNTING CARDS

D0898928

WINNING BLACKJACK

WITHOUT COUNTING CARDS

DAVID S. POPIK

A Carol Paperbacks Book
Published by Carol Publishing Group

First Carol Paperbacks Edition 1992

A Carol Paperbacks Book
Published by Carol Publishing Group
Carol Paperbacks is a registered trademark of Carol Communications, Inc.

Editorial Offices: 600 Madison Avenue, New York, NY 10022
Sales & Distribution Offices: 120 Enterprise Avenue, Secaucus, NJ 07094
In Canada: Canadian Manda Group, P.O. Box 920, Station U, Toronto,
Ontario, M8Z 5P9, Canada

Queries regarding rights and permissions should be addressed to Carol
Publishing Group, 600 Madison Avenue, New York, NY 10022

Manufactured in the United States of America
ISBN 0-8216-2519-5

Carol Publishing Group books are available at special discounts
for bulk purchases, for sales promotions, fund raising, or
educational purposes. Special editions can also be created to
specifications. For details contact: Special Sales Department,
Carol Publishing Group, 120 Enterprise Ave., Secaucus, NJ 07094

10 9 8 7 6 5 4 3 2 1

This book is the culmination of 18 months of an in-depth study of the game of blackjack.

It could not have been accomplished in 18 years without the help of my

wife and daughter,
ROSALIND and ROBERTA

Contents

Preface 9
1. Introduction.. 13
2. Some Time Later... 16
3. Card Counting 20
4. How Atlantic City Blackjack Is Played.............. 24
5. The Basic Strategy 36
6. Insurance, Anyone? 46
7. Basic Strategy Results 49
8. Averages and Probabilities............................. 54
9. Relationship of a Basic Strategy to
   Wins and Losses 60
10. The Gambler's Fallacy.................................. 62
11. Tossing Coins.. 64
12. The Win-Loss Group System......................... 69
13. Basic Betting Progressions 77
14. Advanced Betting Progressions....................... 83
15. When to Stop.. 88
16. Potpourri... 91
    Appendix 99

Contents

Preface

Preface

If you were to jot down the number 2, three times, and total the result, you would have no choice but to agree with me that the sum would be 6.

If many years ago, Roy Rogers asked his horse how much one and one was—and the horse correctly tapped out the answer—after which Roy wrote this down and sent it to the Massachusetts Institute of Technology for safekeeping; and if our first astronaut to land on the moon wrote his lucky number 2 on a piece of moon rock and our government forwarded it to this same institution for possible evaluation; and if some newborn baby drooled onto his pillow in the shape of a 2 and the parents excitedly sent the pillowcase to this same institution to determine the possible significance of this outstanding event; and finally, if some professor took note of the fact that in each case a 2 was involved, and decided to feed all the facts into the most sophisticated computer on hand, the first and most basic fact to emerge would be that the sum of the numbers in these three events is 6.

Despite the variance in time and distance, this total is exactly the same as you would arrive at if you were to jot down the number 2 three times, and add them up. Some things cannot be changed. The hard core, irrefutable percentages of mathematics hold true throughout the game of blackjack as they do throughout everything else in our universe.

If you draw a card instead of standing, or stand instead of drawing—due to myths, superstitions, hunches, or ignorance of proper play; yes, you may win that hand. You may even end up a particular session as a winner. Long-term blackjack percentages, though, would soon overtake short-term good luck.

When you blame another player at the table for making a poor play that you believe was the cause of your lost hand; true, his particular play and your loss did coincide. *But if you truly believe that how this player plays the game affects your overall percentages, read no further; this book is not for you.*

If you are not convinced that you must play the game as if you are playing one-on-one against the dealer, and this book does not persuade you to change your mind, then we have both wasted our time.

Winning Blackjack
Without Counting Cards

CHAPTER 1

Introduction

When I enlisted in the Army Air Corps in the Spring of 1941, the only thing that "21" meant to me was the number of dollars per month that I was to receive as pay. I soon found out that there was another meaning to this number, and for the next two years or so I participated in thousands of hands of the game of blackjack.

The game itself and the jargon used was quite simple, and lacked the sophistication of what is today known as "casino" blackjack. The dealer held the deal until someone other than himself was dealt a blackjack, at which time the deck was passed to this player, and he in turn became the new dealer. There were no rules as to whether or not the dealer should stand or draw, and with a game of six or seven players, the dealer would ponder for some time, examining each hand—with one card faced down—before deciding his own move.

There were very few words used in common with the

language of today's blackjack. To "hit" or "stand" were about the only ones that I seem to recall. There were no splitting of pairs nor doubling down.

One of my fondest memories is that of a grizzled old Master Sergeant who, when becoming the dealer, would impatiently growl to the players to "Shower down . . . like shit from a tall ox," in order to get them to speed up the placing of their bets. A far cry from today's dealers.

That was my experience, until the proximity of Atlantic City beckoned me. Not ever having been in a gambling casino, my wife and I, along with a number of other couples, decided to spend a few days visiting the seashore and exploring the casinos. I armed myself with a basic strategy recommended by some of the experts—no card counting involved—a few hundred dollars, and my confidence, instilled by the assurance of these experts that I could play blackjack at just about an even percentage with the house.

The vacation was fine, but needless to say, I won no money. What really appalled me, though, was that I actually saw very few players walk away from the table as winners. I wandered from table to table trying to observe those that seemed to be winning, but this was either the unluckiest day for blackjack players in the history of gambling, or the experts were misleading us. If there were any card counters at the tables that day, they too were caught in the miasma of bad luck. Even those betting a few hundred dollars at a time were taking a beating. I naively assumed that no one would dare place a bet that large without practicing the art of card counting—and they certainly knew a bit more about the game than just a good basic strategy.

The experts and authors of books on blackjack, with a few exceptions, would get a great kick over the fact that I thought a few hundred dollars constituted a large bet. Many of them reeled off numbers in the four and five figure range and wrote as if these were average bets. It seemed that the only time they would place a bet as small as I witnessed most of the players making, was while waiting for a shoe to turn advantageous to the player—in accordance with whatever card counting system they used. Some books bandied about figures that many of us would like to earn as a year's salary. These figures only tended to make me feel that I had read unrealistic accounts of the game of blackjack.

Along with my family and good health, I am blessed with a few other attributes—three of them being the love of mathematics, extreme patience, and never becoming bored. I can literally sit down and work 12 to 16 hours a day for weeks on end, writing tiny figures into analysis pads and pore over them for whatever results I may happen to find.

This is my forte—and I decided to put it to use with regard to the game of blackjack. What follows are my findings, conclusions, theories and recommendations.

CHAPTER 2

Some Time Later . . .

Well over a year has passed since my initial visit to Atlantic City and my determination to unravel the mysteries of blackjack. I have spent the time involved in an in-depth study of the game—calculating, computing, reading about, and observing the game. Obviously, this was something I enjoyed doing, finding it more of a challenge than seeking monetary gain.

Throughout this time I had often given thought to whether it would be worthwhile to put my findings down on paper. I decided that this would depend entirely on whether or not what I have to say would be of any help to the person who I like to refer to as the "average blackjack player."

My time was spent fruitfully, and as I did what I had originally set out to do, I have gone ahead with my writing.

My main purposes were to find out why most of the players that I observed lost more often than they won, and if I could unearth any information that would increase their chances against the house.

I solved the first problem almost immediately, as it does not take an expert to know poor playing. Most players played the game as if they had no idea that every move they made could increase or decrease the overall house's edge. This acknowledged house's edge, along with how poorly one played, determined the losses suffered over a period of time.

My aim of helping players increase their chances more than by simply following recommended basic strategies developed much later.

Being an avid reader, I decided to obtain as many books and articles about the game that I could lay my hands on. I thoroughly digested seven or eight books, after which I decided to give a cursory examination to any others I might come across before reading each and every word. The reason for my loss of interest was that I found, that except for the fact that some books were more lucid or well-written than others, they all expounded the same major facts: a description and use of a basic strategy, a card-counting system, and money management.

Most of the recommended moves offered as a basic strategy were more or less clones of one another, although all of the books offered valuable information for any blackjack player. The information on card counting ran the gamut from the simplest, such as counting only tens, aces, fives, or any combination thereof, to systems so complex that one would be in need of a photographic memory and a portable computer to make them work as described. The third major portion, money management, was usually a total disaster when it came to advising the non-counter.

As far as I could determine, there was no book written

entirely for the thousands of non-counting blackjack players that daily visit Atlantic City. I thought these players might look forward to a book that does not stress counting as the only means to playing successful blackjack.

My thoughts on blackjack literature are by no means meant to discourage anyone from reading any books or articles on the subject. It seems to me that anyone contemplating playing the game can only benefit from the wealth of information available. Nothing I have written is meant to disparage any author or book, for on the contrary, I found most of the books to be well-written and the authors well-informed.

The non-counting blackjack player must excel in two fields in order to narrow, or best, the house's advantage. One is a basic strategy, which must be memorized and used to its fullest potential. The other is money management.

The former is fairly easy to master, and many players do so and use it successfully. The problems arise in the field of money management. Very few players have the slightest idea of what this area is all about, and as far as I can determine, increase or decrease their bets purely by whim. I feel that the lack of intensive study of this subject by experts of the game is the main cause of players' shortcomings. Most of the information offered on this subject, with regard to betting progressions, places the player in a worse position than *if he were to stick to a one-unit bet throughout the entire session of play.*

For some reason or other most authors feel compelled to offer some sort of betting progression, most to the detriment of the player. Even accomplished card counters often fail to beat the game due to their failure to keep their bets within the proper limits of their bankroll, and the plus or minus situations of the remaining cards in the shoe.

It is in this field of money management that I have discovered what has become the basis of this book. But more about that later.

CHAPTER 3

Card Counting

Although this book is written for the non-counting blackjack player, a brief description of card counting is in order at this point.

The term "card counting" is a misnomer. Except for some of the very simplest systems, during which you may count one or two denominations of cards that have been played, you do not actually count cards. Rather, numbers such as a +1 may be assigned to a 10, a +2 to an ace, and a −1 to some lower cards.

As cards are exposed, the player mentally subtracts or adds these figures to one another and keeps the minus or plus total in mind. As these totals vary, there are changes in the probabilities of winning or losing with the cards that remain in the shoe. Bets are varied accordingly; larger bets if the shoe has shifted in favor of the player and minimum bets when it favors the house or is neutral. As the shoe diminishes in cards, a decided advantage may develop for the player, at which time the bets would be increased in proportion to the advantage detemined by the count, and perhaps some changes from the standard basic strategy.

One can readily see that a single deck, played down to its very end, can enable a player to manipulate his bets as the probabilities vary. On the other hand, playing against eight decks (as used in Atlantic City), can take much longer to change to an advantageous position, if at all. In addition to this drawback, approximately 25 percent of the cards remaining in the shoe is never dealt, but rather all cards are reshuffled. This multi-deck shoe, played only three-quarters of the way down, is but one of the casino's defenses to the card counter.

It struck me as rather strange, and discouraging for the blackjack player, that there was no book that I could locate which did not emphasize some sort of counting system. Although there are definite advantages offered by some of these systems, blackjack remains the only casino game where, even for the non-counter, the player's skill can keep the house's edge to below 1 percent. Except for a few individual bets at some other games, these odds are the best to be found at any game in the casinos.

Why then is the non-counter tolerated by these authors only as a potential counter? No one has previously written a book solely for those who, for an abundance of reasons, do not wish to, or cannot learn, the art of card counting. There are literally thousands of players that could benefit from a pro and con view of a basic strategy, without being put down by the fact that if they fail to learn a counting system their chances of winning are slim.

With an eight-deck shoe being dealt only three-quarters of the way down at Atlantic City casinos, the counter's percentages have diminished considerably, while the non-counter's chances have changed so little as to be almost indistinguishable from playing with a lesser amount of decks.

For those interested in the percentage decrease to a card counter by making a change from playing against one deck as compared to playing against eight decks, a table of comparative percentages can be found in the Appendix.

All books indicated that one could not stay ahead of the game without mastering some form of card counting, but *The Pocket Guide to Gambling*, written by David Spanier (Simon & Schuster, 1980), states that, "It is estimated that one out of 2,000 players is a card counter, and of these perhaps only one in 20 is a winner." And this statement was made before the eight-deck shoes. I firmly believe that a statistic such as this can easily be bettered by a well-versed non-counter.

Perhaps, though, you are one that feels that card counting is the route to take with regard to blackjack. If so, and you have the time and mental energy to master a good system, by all means go for it. Read a few of the best books on the market or attend one of the classes or seminars that are constantly being offered. It is truly the best chance of beating the casinos if you can play against one or two decks, with your chances lessening in direct proportion to the increase in the number of decks the casino uses against you.

In *Turning the Tables on Las Vegas*, written by a blackjack player under the pseudonym of Ian Anderson (Vintage Books, 1978), the nameless author is described on the back cover of the book as, ". . . considered by many to be the best blackjack player in the world." He states, however, that he will play against no more than two decks, and will do so only if a one-deck game is unavailable. Unfortunately, Atlantic City does not offer this desirable condition to the card counter.

Since this book recommends a betting system calculated to gain percentages without counting cards, all percentages, averages, probabilities, and player's actions, from this point on, are meant for the non-counting blackjack player.

CHAPTER 4

How Atlantic City Blackjack Is Played

This chapter may be disregarded by those readers who have been playing the game. I have found, however, that any book I have read has enriched my store of knowledge, and I feel that any reader, novice or expert, may pick up a point or two.

The object of the game of blackjack is to beat the dealer. This can be accomplished in a number of ways:

1. To finish the game with a total higher than the dealer's, but not over 21;
2. To acquire *any* total below 21 and have the dealer "bust"; or
3. To be dealt a blackjack at a time that the dealer has not been dealt a blackjack.

Method of Table Play

- *Table Layout.* The blackjack table is semi-circular, around which one to seven players may be seated on the circular side, with the dealer standing on the straight side. The first seat to the left of the dealer is considered the number one position; the last seat to the dealer's right, the number seven position. There are seven small circles, or boxes, imprinted on the felt top, into which the players must place their bets, each one to be used by the player at a matching seat. On the dealer's side of these circles (or boxes) are two semi-circular lines in which is inscribed the reminder that "insurance pays 2 to 1," and in which area the insurance bets are placed. A card displayed in one corner of the table notes the present table limits and some rules of the game. Limits may be changed after a half-hour notice is verbally given to the players at the table.

- *Starting The Game.* At the discretion of the pit boss, but in most cases not even called to his attention, players may play two or more positions. This is almost always allowed, and usually will not be stopped unless the casino is exceptionally crowded.

    Prior to cards being dealt, players must place their bets in their appropriate spaces. Chips should be stacked one on top of another, with the larger denominations at the bottom, and must not be handled again until after the dealer has completed his own hand and determined the status of the players' hands.

    Cards are dealt out of a container known as a "shoe," which is wired to the table at the extreme left of the dealer.

The shoe is constructed so that the top card is partially hidden from view, and is the only card that can be dealt. Obviously, this is designed to prevent sleight-of-hand maneuvers by the dealers, and to hide, as much as possible, any card imperfections that may be inflicted by wear or a player. This creates an atmosphere of trust, and is mutually protective of both player and house, along with a diminished chance of collusion between a dealer and a player.*

In a similar position to the shoe, at the right side of the dealer and bolted to the table, is an upright container into which the discarded and "burned" cards are placed. (A "burned" card is the top card that is discarded by the dealer after shuffling the decks, and by a new dealer taking over before the shoe is played out.) The burned card is disclosed if requested by a player. Players whose hands stray too close to either the shoe or discard box may be expected to be cautioned by the dealer, and asked to keep their hands at a specified distance from either container.

A yellow cutting card divides the last one-quarter (two decks) of the decks in the shoe from the first three-quarters. After this card appears and the hands in progress are completed, the dealer shuffles all eight decks and offers the cut to the player to whom the cutting card was dealt. If this player refuses to cut, the cards are offered to each player from the dealer's left to his right. The cut is ac-

---

*Despite all precautions, plus the ever-watchful ceiling cameras, two casinos were taken to the tune of an estimated $25,000.00 each, by dealers that were able to press "bumps" into certain cards. These marked cards were evidedntly dealt out to, or held from, the dealer's associates at propitious moments.

complished by inserting the cutting card in the stack of cards at least ten cards from either end. The decks are then placed alongside the shoe, at which time the dealer re-inserts the cutting card into a point indicated by a mark on the side of the shoe that approximately represents the three-quarters of the shoe that will be dealt. The casino, however, may determine after each round of play that the cards should be reshuffled (an action that is very seldom taken, as it is reserved for suspected card counters). The cards are replaced into the shoe, a card burned, and a new deal started.

Card Hands

- *Card Values.* Cards from 2 to 10 are counted at face value. Pictures, sometimes referred to as "face" cards, are counted, and will hereafter be referred to, as 10's. An ace is counted as an 11, and will remain so unless it places the hand in excess of a total of 21. In this case it will then be considered a 1.
- *Blackjack.* A two-card total containing an ace and a 10 (or picture card) is, with one exception, a blackjack. The exception is if a 10 is drawn after splitting aces, or an ace after splitting 10's, which will be discussed in the paragraph on splitting pairs.
- *Soft hand.* A soft hand is one that contains an ace that is counted as an 11 and does not put the total over 21. If it does put the total over 21, it is counted as a 1. For example, if an ace and a 6 are held, it is counted as a 17. If a 9 is then drawn, the total is 16; for if the ace were now counted as an 11, the hand would be over 21.

In the above example you may hear the dealer state "7 or 17." This is more to clarify the hand to the player, than fact. If the player were to stand in this situation, and the dealer's hand ended with a total of 17, the hands would push. In no way may the player's hand total the 7 that the dealer mentioned.

- *Hard hand.* A hard hand is one that does not contain an ace, or if it does, the ace can only be counted as a 1 (to keep the total from exceeding 21).
- *Push.* If both the player and the dealer arrive at completed totals that are the same, the hands are considered a push; a stand-off with no exchange of chips. Players are cautioned that although the hands may push, the chips may not be touched until the dealer has checked the player's cards and noted the push, usually by signalling in the form of tapping the table directly in front of the player's hand.
- *Bust.* If either the player or dealer draws a card, or cards, and the total of the cards exceeds 21, the hand is considered a bust.

Player's Choices

With a few exceptions, the game is conducted by the use of hand signals and actions. If the player would like to draw a card, a "hit" is signalled by motioning a rearward movement, i.e., a short movement from the area in which the bet is placed, toward the player. The dealer, however, will construe many other hand motions as hit signals, such as tapping the table or a downward motion toward the table.

If the player would like to pass, or "stand," the signal

consists of a side-to-side motion. This hand signal has no substitutes.

The rule regarding busts is the prime reason for the house advantage; that is, if a player breaks, the game is lost at once, even though the dealer may likewise break. Unfortunately, the phrase "beat the dealer" does not apply to totals over 21.

Since this bust rule places the player at a tremendous disadvantage, the house offers a bonus to a player who acquires a blackjack, plus certain options that may be exercised to gain additional percentages—options that the dealer does not enjoy. The bonus offered is a pay-off of 150 percent of the player's original bet (if the player is dealt a blackjack), and the options are to allow the player to "split" or "double down," both to be made *after* the cards have been dealt.

• *Splitting Pairs.* If a player is dealt any pair (and keep in mind that a 10 and a face card are considered a pair), these cards may be split. This is accomplished by placing an additional bet, in the same amount as the original one, and playing each of the two cards as if they were individual hands. The player must not touch the cards to separate them, but just places the additional bet alongside the one on the table. The dealer will separate the cards and adjust the chips.

The two hands are played from the dealer's left to his right. If another pair is the result of the first hit, the hand cannot be split again. After *any* second card is dealt to either, or both of the cards of the pair, the hand may be doubled, as noted in the section on "doubling down."

There are two special conditions to note when splitting pairs:

1. If aces are split, only one card is dealt to each ace; and
2. If a 10 is dealt to an ace, or an ace to a 10, the hand is not considered a blackjack, but rather a total of 21.

- *Doubling Down.* This is the option of placing an additional bet on any two-card total, with the exception of a blackjack or a two-card total of 21. This extra bet is likewise set out near the original bet, and once again the dealer adjusts the chips. Only one additional card is dealt to this hand, and is placed sideways on the layout. The original bet does *not* have to be doubled, but any amount *up to* the original bet may be placed.

  I see no reason why a player would bet less than the maximum allowed, for if the hand is worth the additional bet, that bet should be the highest amount possible. The occasion could arise that the player may not have enough chips left to place the maximum bet, in which case betting what is available is still the wisest choice.

  When a 10, comprised of two 5's, is doubled, the player should verbally express the fact that the bet is meant to double down on a 10, and not to split 5's.

  There are occasions when a player will split or double down against a dealer's ace. If the dealer turns a blackjack, *he will only take the player's original bet; the player will retain his extra bet.* Thus, do not hesitate to make these plays when called for by the basic strategy, as the second bet cannot be lost solely because the dealer turns a blackjack.

- *Insurance.* Taking insurance is another extra bet that may be made after the player views his cards, but only when the dealer's up-card is an ace. Each time the dealer shows an ace the player may place an additional bet of *up to* 50 percent of the original bet. This supposedly "insures" against losing to a dealer's possible blackjack.

If the player takes insurance for a full 50 percent of his original bet, while holding a hand other than a blackjack, and the dealer turns a blackjack, the player is paid 2 to 1 on the insurance bet and loses the original bet. Thereby, he breaks even. If the dealer does not turn a blackjack, the player loses the insurance bet, and will win or lose his original bet as the hands are played out in a normal manner.

If the player insures while holding a blackjack, he must come out a winner. In this case, if the dealer turns a blackjack, the player is paid 2 to 1 on the insurance bet and the hands push. If the dealer does not turn a blackjack, the player loses the insurance bet and is paid the usual 3 to 2 for his blackjack.

Insurance bets are paid off, or collected, by the dealer immediately after he discloses his hole card. See the chapter on insurance for a detailed explanation of this bet.

Dealer's Actions

I consider the blackjack dealer's job to be the most strenuous—mentally and physically—of any job at the casino. Dealers, just like anyone or anything, run the gamut from excellent to poor. The better dealers, however, so outnumber the poorer ones, that the average dealer is a very proficient professional.

The dealer must follow very restrictive rules as to how his hand is played. He must hit totals of up to 16 and stand on totals of 17 (soft or hard) and over. He draws no additional cards if his point count will have no effect on the outcome of the round of play.

One can readily see the advantage of knowing the exact plays the dealer must make. This information is invaluable when calculating optimum percentages of players' moves.

- *Blackjack.* If a player holds a blackjack, and the dealer's up-card is a 10 or an ace, the player is passed, with no signal required. If the dealer does not turn a blackjack, this player is paid prior to the dealer completing his own hand. If the dealer does not show a 10 or an ace, the player holding a blackjack is paid at once, no matter what seat he occupies and before any other player receives additional cards.

- *Settling Accounts.* If a player breaks, the dealer takes his bet before continuing on to the next player, unless the hand has been insured. After the dealer plays his own hand, he will pay off winners or take lost bets starting at his right.

Although one may see an impatient dealer pass a player whose cards total an amount that implies the player will stand, such as in the 17 to 20 range, a dealer must wait for the player to signal. This serves a two-fold purpose. It allows players no recourse to claim, after the next card is exposed, that they had intended to signal a hit, and keeps the "ceiling eyes" on possible crooked dealers that may hit or pass a playing cohort due to cards marked by the dealer.

After the first round of cards has been dealt, if a card is accidentally exposed, it remains as the next card to be dealt. It is offered to each player in turn, and may be accepted or refused. If refused, however, the player may not be dealt another card.

I saw one of the super-fast dealers give a 10 to a player that had signalled a pass. The player refused the card, as did every other player at the table. The dealer's up-card was a 3 and his hole card a 10, a total that the rejected card broke. There were two totals of 12 at the table, and whether or not one of these players would have asked for a hit, I don't know, but it is a common move to hit 12 to a dealer's 3. In this case both players (who would have broken if hit), passed, and the dealer had to draw the 10.

I watched one dealer turn up the yellow cutcard, which she had drawn in place of her hole card. This card was carefully and quickly placed under her up-card (as is the procedure). It was not noticed until, much to her surprise, and everyone else's at the table, she was ready to play her hand. The pit boss was called, and he decided that the dealer would take the next card off the shoe. He allowed all players the option of remaining in the game or dropping out and keeping their bets. As the dealer's up-card was a 10, all players but two dropped out. The dealer drew a 6 and then broke.

The pit boss did not have to give the players the choice of dropping out or remaining in the game, but did so purely as a good-will gesture. See the Casino Control Commission rule 19:47-2.15, (e), under "Irregularities," at the end of this chapter.

Many strange situations arise that may not be specifically covered by the rules. In these cases the pit boss is arbitrator. Almost without fail, unless the player is obviously attempting a ploy, he will make a decision that favors the players.

Miscellaneous Definitions

There are a few other terms occasionally referred to throughout the game with which players should be familiar. These include:

- *Basic Strategy*. This term describes a condensed series of actions the player may take to gain optimum percentages from each of the 550 player-dealer card combinations that may appear.
- *Stiff Hand*. This is a hand that can break when hit with just one card, or any hard total of 12 to 16.
- *Toke*. A tip, or gratuity for the dealer. This may be given directly to the dealer or played for him, in which case it would double in amount if the player wins the hand. In order to play the tip, just place the chip, or chips, toward the front part of the circle in which the original bet has been placed. You may remark to the dealer "this is for you," but he already knows this by the position of the chip. The dealer to whom the tip is given does not personally take it, but drops it into a container. The money eventually winds up in a kitty for all dealers on duty for that day.
- *Third Baseman*. The player occupying the seat that is dealt the last hand on the table is sometimes referred to by this phrase. This poor soul is the one blamed for any poor move he may make, after which the dealer hits a winning hand. He is never remembered for a single move, after which the next card breaks the dealer.

Irregularities

Excerpts from the *New Jersey Administrative Code*, Title 19; Subtitle K; Chapter 47-2.15, effective date September

15, 1982. Reprinted by permission of the Casino Control Commission.

- (a) A card found turned upwards in the shoe shall not be used in the game and shall be placed in the discard box.
- (b) A card drawn in error without its face being exposed shall be used as though it were the next card from the shoe.
- (c) After the initial two cards have been dealt to each player and a card is drawn in error and exposed to the players, such card shall be dealt to the players or dealer as though it were the next card from the shoe. Any player refusing to accept such card shall not have any additional cards dealt to him during such round. If the card is refused by the players and the dealer cannot use the card, the card shall be burned.
- (d) If the dealer has 17 and accidentally draws a card for himself, such card shall be burned.
- (e) If the dealer misses dealing his first or second card to himself, the dealer shall continue dealing the first two cards to each player, and then deal the appropriate number of cards to himself.
- (g) If no cards are dealt to the player's hand, the hand is dead and the player shall be included in the next deal. If only one card is dealt to the player's hand, at the player's option, the dealer shall deal the second card to the player after all other players have received a second card.

CHAPTER 5

The Basic Strategy

You have learned how the game is played; you must now learn how to play the game. The cards have been dealt—which means you can hold any one of 55 possible two-card combinations, while the dealer shows one card out of a possible 10. Your hand is one of a formidable 550 player-dealer combinations that you will have to consider. Fortunately, though, a mere five choices will cover all possibilities: hit, stand, double-down, split, and insure. Nine of the 550 combinations are blackjacks against a dealer's up-card of a 2 to a 10 and require no move on your part. This chapter demonstrates how easily the remaining 541 combinations are handled.*

*The average number of cards you will draw is one (to the closest whole number), resulting in a completed hand of three cards. You have a decision to reach after being dealt the first two cards, and once again after you draw your third card. This third card—one out of a possible 10—will multiply the possible combinations of *each* hand to 5,410.

Figure 1 is a detailed chart covering all player-dealer combinations that may appear. The player will hold totals that may be treated differently if they are the result of either two, or three or more cards. The column headed "no. of cards per hand" clarifies player's hands that may otherwise seem ambiguous. If there is no notation in this column, it simply means that the player's hand consists of only two cards, as in the case of doubling down or splitting, or that the proper move is to any number of cards, as it would be to any soft hand of 19 or over.

Stand or Hit

The proper play for 31 of the two-card hands (310 player-dealer combinations) is to stand or hit. These two choices considerably cut down on what at first seems to be an insurmountable problem—how to deal with so many different hands. These moves cover about two-thirds of all two-card hands, and will be made quickly and decisively once you learn the basic strategy.

Doubling Down

Figure 2 is an excerpt from Figure 1 that highlights the doubling-down choice. This move can be made while holding only two cards, and as a result there is no need for a "no. of cards per hand" column. Keep in mind that only one card is received when exercising this option.

These double-down situations account for another 17 two-card hands that may appear (facing one of ten possible

---

And all this solved by one out of only five choices after holding the first two cards, and in most cases, one out of only two choices after drawing the third card.

The Basic Strategy

Figure 1—BASIC STRATEGY FOR 8 DECKS ONLY

PLAYER'S CARDS	ACTION TO DEALER'S UP-CARD				
HARD HANDS (No Pairs)					
	NO. OF CARDS PER HAND	STAND	DOUBLE	SPLIT	HIT
5 to 8		Never			Always
9	2	Never	2 to 6		7 to A
10	2	Never	2 to 9		10 & A
11	2	Never	Always		
9, 10, 11	3 or more	Never			Always
12 to 16	3 or more	2 to 6			7 to A
17 & up		Always			Never
● **HARD HANDS (Pairs)**					
2/2, 3/3 & 6/6				2 to 6	7 to A
7/7				2 to 7	8 to A
8/8				Always	
9/9		7, 10, A		2 to 9 except 7	
● **SOFT HANDS**					
A/A				Always	
A/2			5 & 6		2, 3, 4 & 7 to A
A/3, A/4			4, 5, 6		2, 3, & 7 to A
A/5, A/6			2 to 6		7 to A
A/7		7 & 8	2 to 6		9 to A
Up to 17	3 or more	Never			Always
18	3 or more	9, 10, A			2 to 8
19 & up		Always			Never
	NO. OF CARDS PER HAND	STAND	DOUBLE	SPLIT	HIT

Figure 2 — DOUBLING-DOWN CHART

PLAYER'S CARDS	ACTION TO DEALER'S UP-CARD		
	DOUBLE	STAND	HIT
• HARD HANDS			
9	2 to 6	Never	7 to A
10	2 to 9	Never	10 & A
11	Always	Never	Never
• SOFT HANDS			
A/2	5 & 6	Never	2, 3, 4, & 7 to A
A/3 & A/4	4, 5, 6	Never	2, 3, & 7 to A
A/5 & A/6	2 to 6	Never	7 to A
A/7	2 to 6	7 & 8	9 to A

dealer's up-cards). Once again note how a few decisions can cover your actions against a good portion of the hands that you will be dealt.

Unlike some other recommendations, all of these double-down plays will produce winning hands in excess of 50 percent of the time, but in all cases except one, later noted, the winning percentages are *slightly lower than if you did not double*. This can readily be understood when you realize that if you do not double, and draw a card, you can draw again, whereas you are stuck with the one card you draw when you do double. In all recommended cases, though, the differences are so small, that the winnings from these double-down situations are greater than the winnings from the same hands that are not doubled.

The one exception to a difference in the winning percentage between doubling or drawing, is when you hold an A/6 to a dealer's 2 to 6. In this case, whether or not you decide to double, you will draw only one card; for if you draw an ace, 2, 3, or 4, your hand will total a soft 18 to 21, and if you draw a 5, 6, 7, 8, 9, or 10, your hand will total a hard 12 to 17; all hands that require you to stand against a dealer's 2 to 6.

The recommended double-down options account for an 80 percent gain (on these moves *only*) when these hands are doubled rather than hit. Two-card totals that should be considered for doubling appear 19.5 percent of the time, so the player must be aware of these opportunities.

Splitting Pairs

Six other two-card hands appear (facing one of ten possible dealer's up-cards) that are candidates for the splitting option. These hands do not appear as often as the double-down options, but nevertheless contribute a percentage to the winnings.

Figure 3 is also an excerpt from Figure 1, and highlights the splitting choices. This move, as in doubling down, is likewise allowed while holding only two cards—the pair.

Figure 3 — *SPLITTING-PAIRS CHART*

PLAYER'S CARDS	ACTION TO DEALER'S UP-CARD		
• HARD HANDS	SPLIT	STAND	HIT
2/2, 3/3 & 6/6	2 to 6	Never	7 to A
7/7	2 to 7	Never	8 to A
8/8	Always	Never	Never
9/9	2 to 9 except 7	7, 10, A	Never
• SOFT HANDS			
A/A	Always	Never	Never

Once again there is no need for a "no. of cards per hand" column.

Although the two cards are handled as if they are individual hands, another split is not allowed if another similar card is drawn. The double-down move, however, may be made after one card is drawn.

All proper splitting decisions increase the percentage of winning on playing the single card of the pair as compared to the percentage of winning on the two-card total, but do not necessarily increase this percentage to over 50 percent. But as in the case of hitting a total of 16 against a 9, you may still lose over 50 percent of the time splitting certain pairs, but if you do not split them your losses will be greater.

Many players consider a total of 18 an excellent hand on which to stand. If, however, the 18 is the result of holding two 9's, and you do not split them as recommended, you will be giving up a 70 percent gain on this move—a .25 percent loss on the overall percentage.

Insurance

The preceding charts have accounted for, and have shown how to deal with, 54 out of 55 of the player's two-card hands (540 out of 550 player-dealer combinations) that you may face each time you are dealt a hand. The remaining hand is a blackjack that you will be dealt 4.7 percent of the time, or on an average of about once out of every 21 hands. There is no two-card combination, with the exception of a total of 20, that will appear a greater number of times.

No choice or signal is required when a blackjack faces a dealer's up-card of a 2 to a 10, but when a dealer shows an ace, you may take insurance. I see so many players making this insurance bet that a detailed analysis is in order. I have devoted the next chapter to just that. Please—read this chapter carefully.

Players who have been following popular recommended strategies will immediately notice that I do not recommend hitting a total of 12 to a dealer's up-card of 2. A detailed explanation of this move is outlined in the Appendix.

The players who are always fearful of breaking, and stand on stiff hands that should be hit, should consider the following: the fact that a recommended play may lose more often than it wins does not necessarily mean that the play is wrong. This situation arises constantly during the course of playing blackjack. Not hitting a 16 against a dealer's up-card of a 7 to an ace is probably the most misapplied move of the game. If you hit a 16 against a dealer's up-card of 9 you will lose about 72 percent of the time, whereas if you were to stand, you would lose about 77 percent of the time, a 6.5 percent loss on this particular play. It may hurt to hit, knowing that you will lose most of the time—but *do* it.

Losing at the rate of 72 percent of the time is certainly a stumbling block when trying to convince a player to hit a 16 when it is appropriate to do so. It is only natural to shy away from a move that always seems to be one that loses, but like the clichéd answer to those who are fearful of growing old, ". . . consider the alternative."

Combinations that are recommended to be hit and that will lose over 50 percent of the time are:

> Hard 12 to 16 to dealer's 7 to ace.
> Soft 17 to dealer's 9, 10, and ace.
> Soft 18 to dealer's 10 and ace.

Despite losing more than 50 percent of the time than if you were to hit these hands, you will lose less than if you were to stand.

Figure 4 is a short version of the detailed basic strategy as outlined in Figure 1. This chart can very easily be memorized, while refering back to Figure 1 for any necessary clarification. Although you are permitted to have, and refer to, written material at the table, I believe you will play a more relaxed and better game the more knowledgeable you are about the game.

Plays should be made intuitively and with no hesitation. Fast, proper moves will have no more of a positive effect

Figure 4—CONDENSED BASIC STRATEGY

HARD HANDS	
5 To 8	Always Hit
9, 10 & 11 (3 cards or more)	Always Hit
12 To 16	Stand 2 To 6
17 & Up	Always Stand

DOUBLE DOWN (2 cards only)	
9	2 To 6
10	2 To 9
11	Always
A/2	5 & 6
A/3 & A/4	4, 5 & 6
A/5 To A/7	2 To 6

SPLIT	
2's, 3's & 6's	2 To 6
7's	2 To 7
9's	2 To 9 Except 7
8's & Aces	Always
4's, 5's & 10's	Never

SOFT HANDS	
Up to 17	Always Hit
18	Stand 2 To 8 Hit 9 To A
19 & Up	Always Stand

on the cards you draw than poor plays made by a fellow player will cause more than average losses. Nevertheless, mistakes with regard to basic strategy or money management will be kept to a minimum if these areas are learned thoroughly.

I offer no suggestions on drinking habits, concentration, or how to conduct oneself at the table. Blackjack players are as individualistic as any other segment of our population, so I only caution—know thyself.

CHAPTER 6

Insurance, Anyone?

For the non-counter, unequivocally, *Never!*

If I were asked for a one-word definition of the word "gamble," I would answer "percentages." That is what gambling is all about. The casinos know this very well, or they could not rake in billions of dollars every year. They know it so well that dealers are required, when showing an ace as an up-card, to inquire of all players at the table if they would care to take "insurance."

Splitting pairs, doubling down, and taking insurance are the only times that players are allowed to place additional bets after seeing their cards. I have yet to hear a dealer ask a player if he would like to split or double down. These last two bets, when properly made, add to the player's percentages, and are not in the casino's interests—as is the insurance bet.

When the dealer shows an ace, there are four cards out of 13 that will produce a blackjack, and nine that will

46

not. This simply means that the odds are 9 to 4 that the dealer will not have a blackjack. By offering odds of 8 to 4 (2 to 1), the house will pay out an average of eight units (two for each of the four times that a blackjack was made when the dealer turned a 10) and keep nine units—out of every 13 that was wagered. This is a 7.69 percent advantage to the house on this particular bet. Nothing really wrong by the fact that the bet is offered, but why take it?

I have heard that players insure because they may hold a good hand, a bad hand, and most of all when they hold a blackjack. Nevertheless, no matter what hand you hold when you insure, the house's favorable percentage remains the same.

Most players need no convincing that insurance is really a bad bet—except if holding a blackjack. The examples herein described will show that taking insurance is *always* a bad bet, no matter what hand you may hold.

True enough, when you insure that blackjack, you must win something. If your original bet was $10, and you followed it with a $5 insurance bet, you would come out winning $10 whether or not the dealer turned a blackjack. How can you lose if you always win? Is this a reversal of a "Catch 22" scenario to a positive situation? Not exactly. This is a classic example where constant wins will place you percentages behind.

As there are only four out of every 13 cards that will give the dealer a blackjack (if showing an ace), the simplest way to demonstrate the outcome of taking insurance is to average the results of 13 hands of insured blackjacks.

Let us suppose that you are dealt a blackjack after placing a bet of $10, and then take insurance for $5. The hand can end in one of two ways, with the following results:

1. On an average of four times out of 13 the dealer will turn a blackjack. In such cases the hands will push and the insurance bet will pay $10, for a $40 total win.
2. The remaining nine times the dealer will not turn a blackjack. In these cases, he will take the $5 insurance bet and pay $15 for the blackjack. Once again you will win $10, for a total of $90, and a grand total of $130.

The alternative to this always-win-never-lose situation is *never* to take insurance, no matter what cards you hold. Under the same conditions as above, the results will be as follows:

1. On an average of four times out of 13 the dealer will turn a blackjack. The hands will push, with no pay-out to the dealer.
2. The remaining nine times the dealer will not turn a blackjack. In these cases, the player will be paid $15 for the blackjack (with no loss of a $5 insurance bet), for a total of $135.

This is $5, 3.85 percent more in winnings than if insurance were always taken if the player held a blackjack. In addition to this gain, since one of the cards that the dealer needs is always in the player's hand (a 10), the dealer's chances are further reduced by .24 percent.

CHAPTER 7

Basic Strategy Results

As I had read no books that offered a basic strategy for playing against eight decks, I thought that the lack of this information was the answer to my bewilderment at seeing so many players leaving the tables as losers. I assumed that strategies were being used that were recommended for a lesser amount of decks, and I only needed to calculate a corrected strategy geared to the Atlantic City casino's use of eight decks, and presto! I would discover a method of gaining that elusive percentage over the house.

I was wrong on both accounts. I *did* discover how to gain the extra percentage, explained in detail in later chapters, but not by an improved strategy.

I experienced extreme disappointment when, after tens-of-thousands of calculations, I realized that the few changes I felt should be made to the existing recommended strategies were not enough to make much of a difference.

After further observing hundreds of players, I realized

that I was also wrong as to why there were so many losers; it wasn't a wrong strategy being played, but rather no strategy whatsoever. Even those players that seemed to follow an accepted strategy strayed too often from their know-how to play effectively. I would like to think that most players would make an effort to learn, and properly play the game, prior to taking on the casinos—but that foolish notion has been dispelled.

Basic strategy is like a two-edged sword, and most players were inflicting wounds upon themselves rather than upon the house. Hunches and rash plays were more the order of the day, rather than following a predetermined, recommended strategy. This failure to utilize available knowledge was the prime cause of losses, and *not* the house's small edge. *The player must be bound by specific, recommended rules, as surely as the dealer is bound by house rules.*

Some authors indicated that the basic strategy, as outlined in their particular book, was a compilation of strategies of a number of experts. Others, not as candid, recommended plays so exact to those previously published, that I am certain that they did the same (with regard to a basic strategy, and not to any card-counting systems).

Formulating a strategy from scratch is a formidable task that cannot always be accomplished expeditiously. Many authors may have felt that this area was not the crux of their book, and should be left to others, especially if that information was already widely available. Nor is there anything wrong in doing just that if they had something else to offer, which most did.

This was not so in my case, as an improved basic strategy was the original target of my study. Those readers that are familiar with, and use a good strategy, will notice a number of differences in my table of recommendations. I too took notice of these differences, and as a result gave them an extra bit of attention. I double-checked and rechecked these particular figures, both mathematically and by random sample tests conducted by guidelines outlined by noted statisticians, to insure myself that my final results were correct. Interested readers can find the reason for one of the important differences—standing on a total of 12 to a dealer's up-card of 2 or 3—outlined in the Appendix.

Playing the basic strategy as recommended in this book, you can expect to win an average of 47.5 hands per 100 games, and lose 52.5, excluding pushes.* These figures are extremely close to those that would result if playing a strategy offered by a consensus of others who have studied the game. This simple and basic ratio of wins to losses is only the first of the statistics that affects how you make out at the tables.**

At this point I would like to suggest to those of you with inquisitive minds, and the time and inclination to do so, an experiment involving sets of sample hands: Set up eight decks and deal yourself, or have someone deal you, 500 hands. It need not be at one sitting. One-hundred hands should take about 45 minutes, and you can break the sessions into as many as are convenient to yourself.

Play the basic strategy as outlined in this book. No need to keep track of money won or lost, but jot down how

---

*These figures exclude pushes and are based on 100 hands won or lost, counting splits and doubles as single wins or losses. If pushes were included the total number of hands would be about 109.

**To simplify statistics, all figures demonstrating my findings are rounded out to the largest decimal or whole figure that effectively illustrates a point.

many hands are played and each hand won, counting doubles and splits as single wins and disregarding pushes. When finished playing 500 hands, divide the number of winning hands by five. You will be amazed at how close these hands average out 47.5, with even so small a representative set of samples.

But on to further facts. To the 47.5 wins per 100 we can add the expected number of blackjacks—that pay a 50 percent bonus—and gains made by doubling down and splitting pairs, which average out to over four units of our basic bet, totalling winnings to within 1 percent of losses. This places the house at about a .4 to .8 percent advantage, and just about the best odds that can be expected when playing a perfect game with no variation in the amount of the bet.

If any reader, however, has learned a basic strategy offered in any good book published on blackjack, without even bothering to read the major portion of the book devoted to card counting, this house edge of less than 1 percent comes as no revelation.

So why another book? Simply because, as previously noted, I have found no book that offered an in-depth study of anything other than card counting that could possibly negate the house's edge, or offer the slightest hint as to how a player can actually gain a percentage over the house.

Winning betting progressions, as poor as most of them are, are offered because readers demand and expect them to appear in any book on blackjack. They can never change long-play percentages, but *will* result in greater winnings during any winning streak than if just betting single-unit bets. Unfortunately, many more of the bets raised in anticipation of the next winning hand are lost rather than won. There are not enough consecutive winning hands as compared to a losing hand that follows a win.

There are, what appear to be mathematically sound progressive betting systems, but these are severely limited by the player's bankroll and the table's betting limits.

CHAPTER 8

Averages and Probabilities

Average; noun. A number that typifies a set of numbers of which it is a function; a representative type.

Probability; noun. The condition of being probable; a number expressing the likelihood of occurrence of a specific event.

These are two common words with which we are all familiar and constantly use. Throughout this book, however, I use, abuse, and bandy about these words so often that I would like to expand on the dictionary versions.

Basic strategy and money management are both based on probabilities, arrived at by averaging calculated statistics. As these two areas are what this book is all about, I want no reader to misconstrue my figures and percentages.

The U.S. Census Bureau issued a report containing the fact that the average American family had two and one-quarter children. The "average" family may well have two and one-quarter children, but the "probability" of producing this family is nil.

The key words in the definition of "average" are "typifies" and "representative." I have mentioned the "average blackjack player," but such a person is no more to be found than that unfortunate one-quarter of a child that the average family reported to the Census Bureau. Although figures are usually arrived at by what is commonly referred to as "the law of averages," there are no local police or casino security personnel that will enforce this law.

The point that I am trying to stress as strongly as possible, is that even though the averages herein quoted are as accurate as mathematical computations and approved methods of testing can make them, you will probably very seldom, if ever, arrive at an exact average.

Random sampling is an accepted basis for arriving at probabilities, as opposed to repeatedly tossing a coin for an infinite number of times. A standard experiment could be to conduct 200 samplings of 100 tosses of a coin, all repeated under identical conditions. Based on these samplings, we could arrive at probabilities as to how many heads or tails can be expected to fall, the average number of consecutive heads or tails, and whether or not the coin is balanced. If unbalanced, we would know to what extent, as we would be able to predict the percentage of heads and tails to one another.

Any one of these 200 samplings, starting with the very first, could possibly produce the averages that our probabilities predict, but this one sample can have no bearing on the overall probabilities. Properly conducted, the group of samplings would produce results that are as acceptable and conclusive as those that would result if the experiments were conducted ad infinitum.

The occasional blackjack player likewise could possibly arrive at a probable average during one session of play, or in contrast, play hands that reflect the widest divergence from predicted probabilities. It takes the player that is constantly at the game to "average out." This is not meant to discourage the occasional player, for even if playing only once every few months, following a basic strategy based on probabilities calculated for the casino rules is still the best move.

The casinos, of course, are the only true recipients of probability statistics, for only they play endlessly.

One of the bases of this book, and a fact on which I continually keep harping, is that you will average out over an extended period of play. This "averaging out" does not refer to your bankroll, but rather to predetermined percentages, or the odds.

How long it will take to average out depends on whether we are discussing the entire game of blackjack or particular moves. The percentage of breaking when hitting a total of 16 would certainly average out much sooner per number of hands played, than would the percentage of the results of splitting 2's against a dealer's 6. Both facts, of course, can easily be calculated mathematically. But in actual play the length of time it may take to average out a particular action, or the entire basic strategy being played, affects neither winning nor losing during one playing session. Standing on a total of 16 against a dealer's 7 to ace may put a player ahead for that move or session of play, but in the long run the percentages would beat him.

A simple demonstration to prove the averaging-out theory would be to divide a deck of cards into four units of 13 cards each. How many of these units will contain exactly one ace? As we turn them over we may find any amount from no aces to four aces in any single unit. The probability, however, of finding more than one ace in any unit is greater than finding one ace in each unit, which is the average.

In any event, by the time the fourth unit has been turned over, all four aces will have appeared. This total of four, divided by four (the number of units of 13 cards each), will produce an average of one ace out of each unit of 13 cards.

What can we bet in this situation, if we were asked to guess the average number of aces in each unit? Certainly the farm and bank account, as the result was a foregone conclusion. On the other hand, however, although the average number of aces in each unit is one, how many bundles contain this exact average? This bet requires a bit more calculating before we wager any money, let alone the farm. The odds of picking units that contain exactly one ace are slim.

If we were to keep making units of 13 cards each, but only off the top of the deck, and then reshuffling, the odds would remain the same. In the first case, however, the average was determined as quickly as it took to turn over the units, and as often as this demonstration was repeated, the results would appear in the same amount of time.

The demonstration of reshuffling after each unit of 13 cards was dealt would likewise result in the *exact same average, but over an extremely longer period of time*, requiring the dealing of many more units. This latter demonstration reflects the game of blackjack more closely than the first example. In other words, a winning session or move does not necessarily prove a properly played game.

Another averaging-out demonstration would be similar to those you constantly see in print with regard to crimes or accidents that occur every specified number of seconds. If we were to take any number of decks, combined and shuffled, we can make the same kind of statement, i.e., that an ace will appear every 13 cards.

We all accept these statements as fact, and yet are aware that these events do not really occur at the intervals indicated. Not only are the odds highly against turning over an ace every 13 cards, but we would very seldom see even two aces dealt out exactly 13 cards apart. But if we were to count the aces after all the cards were turned, we would once again have turned four aces if we used one deck, eight aces if we used two decks, and so on; arriving at our average of one ace out of every 13 cards turned over.

The odds in all cases are 12 to 1 that one ace will appear every 13 cards turned over. If the dealer were to give you odds as close as 11.9 to 1, the long-play, losing results, would be predestined.

Blackjack is a comparatively slow-moving game. The successful player must be willing to bet and play with the knowledge that averages and probabilities are what determine long-play wins and losses. Luck and haphazardly raising the amounts wagered may result in some winning sessions, but good luck is ground to mincemeat when compared to betting the probabilities.

Aside from the casinos' tremendous profits from having the odds, no matter how small, in their favor, just think of those giants of finance—the insurance companies. With no gambling tables or slot machines, with nothing of intrinsic value to sell, they have legalized gambling in every state of the union (with no referendum from the voters), by the simple means of actuary tables.

I am well aware that prohibitive odds will not discourage gambling. One Canadian lottery, for example, with a top prize of over 11 million (American) dollars, sold to 11 million inhabitants (44 percent of the population), even though the odds against winning were 13,983,916 to 1.

These lottery ticket buyers, along with most other gamblers, had no choice to raise or lower the odds. True, buying two tickets would halve the odds, but at twice the expense, just as the horse player that plays a long shot reduces the probability of winning as compared to playing a favorite. The lottery player had to raise his bet while the horse player had to reduce his chances. Not really a case of manipulating the odds, as probabilities versus dollars just changed in direct proportion to one another.

But the game of blackjack provides the player with many choices, over many combinations of hands, that actually affect the player's overall percentages. This, perhaps, is the reason that the game is first in popularity at the casinos—this choice over one's destiny at the tables.

Unfortunately, though, most players, for reasons best known to themselves, refuse to believe or follow the "actuary charts" of blackjack—the basic strategy, and simply enhance the house's edge at the expense of their own.

CHAPTER 9

Relationship of a Basic Strategy to Wins and Losses

The considerable amount of time that I had spent seeking a winning basic strategy was apportioned between mathematically calculating percentages and proving out the results by actually playing the game of blackjack. Playing was accomplished using both four and eight decks; actually using the cards and also playing against a computer. Full games were played dealt against one, three, and six players. All aspects were carefully documented and averages noted.

There were literally tens-of-thousands of percentages that were amassed during this study of the game. Only those necessary to explain or make a point will be presented—and then only as close to whole figures that will not distort the results.

I was not particularly seeking information other than an improved strategy for playing against eight decks. However, after about 15,000 hands were played—scrupulously following the basic strategy as outlined in Figure 1, I started to notice (and at first was surprised by) a very definite relationship forming between playing this basic strategy and the proportion of wins and losses to each other. Interestingly enough, this same pattern continued for many more tens-of-thousands of games, and with every 5,000 hands or so averaged into my existing percentages, the figures tightened and proved out over and over again.

My surprise turned to satisfaction when I realized that this area was sorely neglected throughout the study of black-jack. My study showed that *for a specific, unfaltering basic strategy, there is a definite relationship between wins and losses, and the lengths of winning and losing streaks.*

CHAPTER 10

The Gambler's Fallacy

Statisticians are fond of describing what has become known as the "Gambler's Fallacy." This is betting on the premise that it is time for a change in a sequence of events, e.g., after a repeatedly tossed coin has turned up as a head many times in a row, it is now due to turn up as a tail. This is, quite truly, a betting system doomed to failure. This theory extends to the turn of a card, the toss of a die, the spin of a roulette wheel, and just about all gaming and sporting events.

A perfectly balanced, repeatedly tossed coin, has a 50-50 chance of settling as a head or tail the very first time tossed as it would the one-hundredth time—after turning up as a head for the previous 99 times. The gambler that wagers more than even money to the contrary has fallen into the "Gambler's Fallacy" trap, and has handed his opponent the edge. The blackjack player that raises his bet for no other reason than that he has lost a number of consecutive hands, is guilty of the same error. He has further advanced the bane of casino gamblers—the house's edge.

"It's time for a change" is a poor excuse for a proper money-management plan.

CHAPTER 11

Tossing Coins

The simplest way to demonstrate probabilities is a brief study of tossing coins. Notes can be made of the results of a million tosses, or arrived at by the relatively easy way—random samplings of predetermined numbers. Both methods would result in statistics accurate enough for all practical purposes.

So let's visit a coin-tossing casino.

The first table we stop at advertises that a perfectly balanced coin is being tossed by a robot, with the exact same momentum to each toss. Figure 5 shows the exact number of heads or tails we can expect to fall every 100 tosses, how many heads or tails will fall consecutively, and the probabilities of how often we can expect these groups of consecutive heads or tails to fall every 100 tosses, if at all.

These calculated statistics can be expected to average out more accurately the longer we play. *And you can bet on that!* Keep in mind, though, the two and one-quarter child. No matter how long we play, the chances are slim

Figure 5 — 50-50 PROBABILITY CHART

GROUPS OF	HEADS OR TAILS	REMAINING GROUPS	HEADS PER 100	TAILS PER 100	CHANCE OF EITHER (1 OUT OF)
1	12.5	12.5	12.5	12.5	8
2	6.25	6.25	12.5	12.5	16
3	3.125	3.125	9.375	9.375	32
4	1.5625	1.5625	6.25	6.25	64
5	.7813	.7813	3.9065	3.9065	128
6	.3906	.3906	2.3436	2.3436	256
7	.1953	.1953	1.3671	1.3671	512
8	.0977	.0977	.7816	.7816	1,024
9	.0488	.0488	.4392	.4392	2,048
10	.0244	.0244	.244	.244	4,096
11 AND OVER	.0244	.0244	.293	.293	11/8,192 12/16,384 13/32,768
TOTALS	25.0000	25.0000	50.0000	50.0000	

that any one session of 100 tosses would produce average results.

Any consecutive amount of heads or tails falling (including a single) will hereafter be referred to as a "group." Every 100 tosses can have (theoretically) from one to 50 individual groups of either heads or tails. In reality, though, this figure of "one to 50" is 19 to 31—or within 25 percent of the 25 groups noted in Figure 5.* For this study only groups of one to ten will be considered, as groups of 11 and over fall so seldom that they have little bearing on our averages.

The figures in the column of "remaining groups" are prime factors when determining when to vary the amount of a bet in order to gain a percentage. We must know, e.g., if a change in the amount of a bet is being considered after three consecutive heads have fallen, the total of groups of four or more consecutive heads.

Figure 5 discloses the following:
Total groups of heads and tails combined.......   50
Total number of tosses..............................   100
Average number of consecutive heads or tails ..   2

Knowing this average of two consecutive heads or tails, it seems that all we would have to do is bet on a tail after two heads have appeared, or vice versa, and we would beat the game. What would be the result if this is what we did?

Examining the chart, we find that groups of two appear 6.25 times per 100 tosses, and the *total* of all groups of three or more is the same figure. This simply means that a bet placed in anticipation of a change after two heads or tails

---

*A breakdown of these figures may be found in the Appendix.

have fallen, will be won the 6.25 times that the group remains as a group of two and will be lost the 6.25 times that the two consecutive falls continue on to becoming a longer group. *Any* bet placed at any instance in this game, has a 50-50 chance of being won or lost.

Games similar to this can never be found in a casino unless the odds were somehow tilted in favor of the house. Casinos do not gamble. All games must pay off certain minimum percentages. Just how much of a return a casino will receive on its investment depends on the same factors that affect any business; the number of customers it can attract and the cost of doing business.

Although the table we stopped at does have a balanced coin being tossed, the pay-off is not. In order for the house to gain a percentage over the player, it is paying off at only 90 percent of the amount wagered. We find this percentage too great in the house's favor and decide to skip this game. So on to the next table.

Here we find no notation of a perfectly balanced coin. We spend the time to evaluate this game and find that the coin is falling on an average of 45 heads to every 100 tosses. We would like to wager that the coin falls tails, but tails belongs to the house, and we can only bet on heads.

To sweeten the pot, though, the cloth that the coin falls on has a line drawn across the center that comprises 10 percent of the area. If we win the toss, and the coin touches this line, the house will pay 2 to 1 (to offset a bit of the unbalanced coin). This amounts to a 10 percent bonus on all heads that fall.

Armed with the knowledge of the groups of consecutive heads and tails, we go back to our calculator. We find that even with this extra pay-off, we would still be playing a very small percentage behind the house, *if always placing single-unit bets.* *

But we came to gamble, and this is the most exciting game in town, in addition to offering the best odds. Lady luck constantly floats around the casino, and now and then settles on a player's shoulder. Despite the small favorable house's percentage, we *can* come out a winner. Bear in mind, though, that this is but one session of play, and no way can we continue to stay ahead of the game playing against odds that favor the house.

I truly believe that all blackjack players are aware of the house's edge. So why are there so many of them? The total number of blackjack tables in Atlantic City is twice that of all other table games combined. The only conclusion I can draw concerning anyone playing the game without bothering to learn and utilize every opportunity to gain a percentage, is that such a person is willing to pay to play.

> Good Luck is the gayest of all gay girls,
> Long in one place she will not stay,
> Back from your brow she strokes the curls,
> Kisses you quick and flies away.
>
> But Madame Bad Luck soberly comes . . .
> Sits by your bed, and brings her knitting.

—John Hay

---

*The chapter on the win-loss group theory demonstrates how further calculations pin-point certain instances that an increased bet will actually place the player at an advantage over the house.

CHAPTER 12

The Win-Loss Group System

The situation of the inherent house's edge emphasized the fact that, in a neutral deck, prior to the very first card of any single hand being dealt, the odds are usually against the player. Therefore, to raise a bet purely by whim is a classic example of a "Gambler Fallacy" play.

After the very first card of the hand is out the odds change, but unfortunately, except for splitting or doubling down, the bet can no longer be changed. You can, however, raise or lower a bet in *anticipation* of certain average percentages of wins and losses, as herein outlined.

If tossing a perfectly balanced coin, the chance of tossing 11 consecutive heads or tails is one out of 8,192. In the game of blackjack, the chance of 11 consecutive winning hands is about one out of 10,400. Although we see longer winning streaks, those of 11 and over have been combined into one figure. These combined winning (or losing) groups do not affect any statistics of either Figures 5 or 6.

Reviewing a few facts of a 50-50 probability situation as outlined in Figure 5 (in the chapter on tossing coins), we find:

1. All groups of consecutive heads or tails have similar figures in all columns;
2. Equal amounts in the groups of consecutive heads or tails, including the totals of 25; and,
3. Totals of heads or tails per 100 50
   Divided by the total of groups of consecutive heads or tails .... <u>25</u>
   Equals an average of consecutive heads or tails of 2

Due to the house's edge, in the game of blackjack the number of consecutive wins and losses is not the same as it would be if tossing that perfectly balanced coin. Since each group of consecutive winning hands is, naturally, followed by a group of consecutive losing hands, and vice versa, the number of groups is equal, whereas the amounts of wins or losses in these groups are not equal.

If a chart similar to Figure 5 were drawn up for the game of blackjack, a few of the pertinent facts would look very close to those shown in Figure 6.*

We find similarities in the compositions of Figures 5 and 6, but differences in resulting figures:

---

*All figures disregard pushes and count splits and doubles as single hands. A hand that is split, after which one hand is lost and one hand is won, is considered a push. If you won two consecutive hands, pushed the third hand and won the fourth, it would be considered three consecutive winning hands.

Figure 6.

GROUPS OF	WINS	REMAINING GROUPS	WINS PER 100	LOSSES	REMAINING GROUPS	LOSSES PER 100
1	12.75	12		11.75	13	
TOTALS	24.75		47.5	24.75		52.5

1. All groups of consecutive wins and losses show *different* figures in all columns;

2. Unequal amounts in the groups of consecutive wins and losses, but the totals of these groups are the same: 24.75 (as compared to 25 in Figure 5);* and

3. Total of wins per 100 .... 47.5
   Divided by the total of groups of consecutive winning hands .... <u>24.75</u>
   Equals an average of consecutive winning hands of 1.92

4. Total of losses per 100 .... 52.5
   Divided by the total of groups of consecutive losing hands .... <u>24.75</u>

---

*The unbalance in the favor of the house creates longer losing streaks; thereby a smaller number of total groups of consecutive losses or wins, e.g., if the game were so unbalanced as to produce 99 losses and one win, we could have *no more* than three groups, such as: 60-1-39, 5-1-94, 99-1, etc. Therefore, the more unbalanced the game, the smaller the number of groups. Totals can range from one to 50 groups of consecutive wins or losses. A breakdown of groups can be found in the Appendix.

Equals an average of consecutive losing hands
of 2.12

This average number of less than two consecutive winning hands is hardly enough of a winning streak to stay ahead of the game by progressively increasing one's bets after winning hands. And yet this is exactly what many experts recommend and what you see many players constantly doing.

With so small an average of consecutive winning hands (any 100 hands, though, can produce consecutive wins and losses of any amount), it would seem that there would be no opportunity to increase the amount of a bet without further advancing the house's edge. This is not so.

Figure 6 shows an average of 12.75 single winning hands and an average of 11.75 single losing hands. These figures may at first appear to be incongruous. Why should there be more wins than losses, in any group, in a game where the odds favor the house?

This situation arises only in the groups of one or two consecutive wins or losses. Since the odds do favor the house, winning streaks of three or more consecutive winning hands are shorter than those shown in Figure 5 (a 50-50 odds chart). This results in the one and two groups of consecutive winning hands being longer than if the odds were even. In other words, there are more single winning hands that *do not* continue on to become longer winning streaks.

We also see that there are 24.75 consecutive winning groups, including a single win. In this group of one, the second bet had to be lost in order for the hand to remain a single winning hand. Figure 6 shows that there are about 12.75 single wins. During the remaining 12, longer, winning streaks, the second bet is won, resulting in the following:

Second bets lost..................................	12.75
Second bets won..................................	<u>12.00</u>
Units lost per 100 hands	.75

It would appear that each bet that is made after winning the first hand (after a loss) results in this .75 percent loss. In the game of blackjack, however, in order to keep it from becoming a complete rout of the player, adjustments are made in the forms of the 50 percent bonus for the player's blackjack, and allowing splits and doubles. These advantages add about 4.3 units to the number of units gained by the player's winning hands, or about 9 percent.*

This gain is not quite enough to place the player in an even position with the house, but using the 12.75-loss and 12-win example, it is enough to change the 12-unit win to a 13.08-unit win, thereby *gaining a percentage over the 12.75-unit loss.*

This example demonstrates the foundation of·a simple system that allows the player to actually *gain a percentage over the house.*

Both units and dollars are used to demonstrate various examples, whichever seems appropriate to the situation. A unit is readily converted to any basic amount the reader may wish to wager, whereas simple mathematical calculations are better illustrated by the use of dollars. To further

---

*This figure of 9 percent (or 4.3 units) that is added to units that are won is the final result of many calculations. Many splits and doubles are lost. These losses are added to units that are lost, while winning splits and doubles, plus the blackjacks bonus, are added to units that are won. The 9 percent represents the difference between wins and losses.

simplify examples, basic bets of $5 and $10 are used, which likewise are easily converted to a player's bankroll.

If the player were not given the blackjack bonus and other favorable options, then due to the "unbalanced coin" analogy, at no point—either after a win or a loss—would the odds favor raising a bet. The 9 percent average increase (the player's gain from the blackjack bonus and the split and double options), however, added to the player's hands that are won, in certain cases places the player in a very favorable position.

Study shows that there are instances in the win-loss proportions (similar to the 12.75-loss-12-win example previously demonstrated), where the next-win probability is so close to the next-loss probability, that the 9 percent average increase makes them prime choices for bet increases. These opportunities mainly arise *after the first winning hand* (after a loss) and *after the third consecutive loss.* *

Winning streaks are always in the making. If the bet wasn't increased during a winning streak, the player most likely would feel cheated, and would probably hear another player grumble, ". . . if I were betting you'd really see some winnings." Agreed, this winning streak did not produce the revenue promised by most of the touted progressive betting systems, and money surely would have been made on it had bets been increased.

To further lessen the disappointment at not having increased your bets during a series of consecutive winning hands, bear in mind that three consecutive wins can be expected on an average of only once in about 32 hands;

---

*There are certain other instances during losing streaks where a raised bet would be advantageous, but more than one raised bet during a winning *or* losing streak will cause the plus percentages to erode. If the first raised bet is lost, you *mus* fall back to the one-unit bet.

four consecutive wins once in about 76 hands; six consecutive wins once in about 325 hands, and ten consecutive wins once in about 5,200 hands.*

The average run of consecutive winning hands is slightly less than two, and although more money would have been won on the winning streak noted above if bets had been raised, the following would result if you utilized even a very conservative progressive betting system such as one, two, and three units.

Groups of two consecutive winning hands, after which the third bet is lost............................	6.33
Total groups of three or more consecutive winning hands, after which the third bet is won..	5.6
Units lost per 100 hands	.73

This figure of .73 lost units represents a loss of the third bet of 13 percent more times than this bet is won. The progressive bet of three units at this point only compounds the loss.

According to most experts, raising a bet after a losing hand is a definite no-no (except in cases of certain progressive betting systems calculated for losing streaks), and also might be construed as yet another "Gambler Fallacy" example. There are statistics at work, however, that are unique only to the game of blackjack.

For a clearer picture of how a raised bet after a loss can be turned to the player's advantage, consider the following: Playing the basic strategy as outlined in this book, you can expect to average about 3.6 three-loss groups per

---

*These figures take into consideration the house's edge, and assume that the player is playing a perfect strategy.

100 hands, and about the same number of *four or more* consecutive losses.

If the bet is raised after suffering three consecutive losses, it will be won or lost as follows:

1. The raised bet will be won the 3.6 times that the three consecutive losses remain as three-loss groups; or

2. The raised bet will be lost the number of times that the three consecutive losses continue on to becoming loss groups of four or more consecutive losses.

As in the 12.75-loss-12-win example, the three-loss groups are extremely close in number to the four-or-more-loss groups. As a result, with the 9 percent average gain added to the winning hands, *each increase of one unit to a bet placed after three consecutive losses, plus the same increase after the first winning hand (after a loss), will result in an overall gain of about .5 percent.**

I would like to remind the reader that the 3.6 three-loss group used in the preceding example, is an *average* per 100 hands. Those readers that are going to take my suggestion of playing and recording wins and losses during 500 hands, would do well to note the number of three consecutive losses that appear. Although 500 hands are not really a sufficient amount to use in averaging out a win or loss group, the 3.6 group of three consecutive losses is a figure extremely close to what you will record.

---

*To differentiate between a one-unit bet and an increased bet, the former will be referred to as a "base bet." This bet will not vary as often as the raised bet. Therefore, situations will arise where the progressions consist of one unit and three units; one unit and five units, or any combinations thereof. The difference between these two bets will hereafter be referred to as a "ratio." The numerical differences of ratios are explained in the following chapter.

CHAPTER 13

Basic Betting Progressions

To gain the .5 percent, the one-unit bet is raised only as indicated, and *at no other time*. Although what follows may sound like an Abbott and Costello dialogue, the graphically illustrated progressions should clear things up.

- If the bet that is made after the first win (after a loss) is successful, immediately revert back to a one-unit bet. Continue betting one unit no matter how long the winning streak may last.
- If the bet placed after the third loss is successful, it is considered a first win. This win is to be followed by another second ratio bet.

First Win

• A winning streak where "W" is the first win after a loss and is a single-unit bet:

W(1) - 2 - 1 - 1 - 1 - 1 - etc.

Notice that the first bet after a winning hand is a two-unit bet (or any second ratio bet), followed by single-unit bets. This is a typical example of losing out on winning streaks, but these streaks are few and far between, and most of the time these one-unit bets would be lost, just as they would be if they had been raised.

First Loss

• A losing streak where "L" is the first loss after two or more winning hands and is a single-unit bet:

L(1) - 1 - 1 - 2 - 1 - 1 - 1 - 1 - 1 - etc.

Here we see the bet raised after the third loss. This bet is lost. As a result the following bet has reverted to a single-unit bet, and remains a single-unit bet.

• A losing streak where "L" is the first loss after a single winning hand:

L(2) - 1 - 1 - 2 - 1 - 1 - 1 - 1 - 1 - etc.

This example is the same as the previous one with the exception of the first bet. This is a two-unit bet because it followed a single winning hand, that is, one that was not part of a winning streak.

Note that the raised bet after a third loss is accom-

plished only once during a losing streak, and not after every three losses.
* The following is a combination of the two preceeding "first loss" examples; a losing streak (first set of brackets) that has turned into a winning streak (second set of brackets). "L" is the first loss after either a single or multiple win, hence the [1 or 2] bet.

(L[1 or 2] - 1 - 1 - 2) - (2 - 1 - 1 - etc.)

This is the only time that two raised bets follow one another. The raised bet after the third loss was won. Thereby, it was considered the first winning hand and followed by the second raised bet.

Playing this betting progression and the recommended basic strategy will result in about a .5 percent gain for *each unit wagered in addition to the lowest unit bet*.

The basic strategy has placed the player at less than a 1 percent (approximately .4 to .8 percent) disadvantage if wagering only one-unit bets. An additional increase, as recommended (one unit), will almost even out the odds. A two-unit increase will actually result in an edge over the house.

Dropping this anticipated edge, and assuming that the two-unit increase places the player exactly even with the house, a three-unit increase would place the player at a .5 percent advantage; four units at a 1 percent advantage; six units at a 2 percent advantage, and a ten-unit increase at a 4 percent advantage.

All increases are in addition to the one-unit basic bet. A second-bet *total* of four units will be considered a ratio of 1 to 4; a second-bet total of six units as a ratio of 1 to 6, etc

The obvious question now arises as to why we do not simply play a ratio of, say, 1 to 7, gain a 2 percent advantage, and let the averages just "average out?" This can well be done, but first we should examine a few facts.

Take the player with a $200 bankroll. Playing a $5 to $35 (1 to 7) ratio, this player would enjoy about a 2 percent edge. To fully utilize the basic strategy he must be prepared to double or split the $35 bet when called to do so by proper strategy, and possibly further increase this bet to $105 or $140, as when doubling down after a split. These are hardly prudent amounts to place in jeopardy for this size stake, and a ratio that could quickly spell disaster if used at the start of play.

On the higher end of the spectrum of the "average blackjack player," let us examine the player backed by $1,000. Although I have yet to see this amount of money in front of a player who is making minimum bets of only $5, we will asume that this is exactly what he is willing to do in order to gain a percentage over the house.

The 2 percent gained by the 1 to 7 ratio, if being won at an *exact* average rate (not likely, but makes a point), would produce winnings of 2 percent of the average amount wagered during 100 hands of play. Since the total of the $5 and $35 bets average out to $1,460, the winnings would average out to $29.20 each 100 hands. I do not believe that this player would continue at this rate without arbitrarily raising the amounts of the bets.

Then why not begin to play with a 1 to 23 ratio and a 10 percent advantage? This ratio, using as little as a $5 base bet, would mean that the larger bet would be $115. The player would place himself in the same position as the player with the $200 bankroll. This $115 larger bet would be, in many cases, escalated to $230, and occasionally to $345 or $460.

I recommend starting ratios as indicated in Figure 7.

Figure 7

STARTING RATIOS AND BASE BETS

	STAKE	RATIO	BASE BET
CONSERVATIVE	$ 300	1 to 2	$ 5
	500	1 to 2	5
	1,000	1 to 3	10
	2,500	1 to 3	25
AGGRESSIVE	$ 500	1 to 3	5
	1,000	1 to 3	15
		1 to 4	10
	2,500	1 to 4	25
		1 to 5	25

This precaution against starting play with a ratio that is too large serves a two-fold purpose. First, it minimizes losses if the player falls behind immediately. Second, it keeps all bets in proportion to the player's bankroll. This does not mean that the starting ratio should be 1 to 2, or that the base bet should be $5, but rather that all bets should be made with an eye on the amount of money that the player has on hand.

Figure 7 shows various ratios and base bets with regard to starting stakes. Since the greater the degree of difference between the first (base) bet of the ratio and the second (higher) bet determines the aggressiveness of the wagering, the higher ratios are assigned to larger bankrolls. The larger the bankroll, the more the player can risk at the start of the game.

Although the base bets noted may seem fairly small when compared to the starting stakes, the larger ratio bets will be placed at an average of 32 times per 100 hands (pushes excluded). These amounts, in proportion to the starting stakes, are far from small. For example, take the $500 stake and the 1 to 3 ratio. Thirty-two percent of the time the bet would be a minimum of $15, very often raised to $30 when splitting or doubling down, and occasionally doubled again after splitting to $45 and $60. These size bets are fine if winning and playing with the house's money, but could prove disastrous if losing.

No need to study intermediate or larger bankrolls, as these starting progressions can easily be converted to any amount with which you may begin play. Bear in mind that these ratios and base bets are to be used only when you start to play, are even, or losing. Larger base bets and ratios will be discussed in the following chapter.

CHAPTER 14

Advanced Betting Progressions

Small bets with your own money and larger bets with the house's money.

The base bets and ratios should vary when you are winning, but never when you are losing. We will discuss the latter first—as it is quite cut and dried.

Never raise your starting bets or ratios in an attempt to recoup losses. Bear in mind that you are playing just about even with the house, and many times a bit ahead (depending on the starting ratio). As slowly or quickly that money is lost, it can rebuild again. If playing time seems to be running short, quit playing rather than raise your bets. The practice of chasing after lost money usually results in further losses. No matter what you may feel is the cause of your losses, raising your basic bet will not change this

83

"cause." A "cold" table will not turn "hot" and bad luck will not revert to good luck, just because you doubled your bet.

When to Raise the Bet

Systematically raising bets should be done only if you are running ahead—and then only according to predetermined formulas calculated to conform with your own bankroll and what you expect from playing the game. This means that you should know how much you are ahead, but not an amount so exact that counting your winnings proves to be a distraction. The easiest method of keeping a count of money is by keeping equal stacks of chips totalling equal and specific amounts, and perhaps keeping your original stake separated.

For the purpose of raising bets we will consider being ahead as winnings of at least the larger ratio bets as noted in Figure 8. Under these conditions, if this larger bet is lost, you will not fall below the original stake.

How to Raise the Bet

A conservative formula for a winning situation with a $500 stake would be to raise your bet to 15 percent of your winnings, with a minimum ratio of 1 to 4. This means that if your base bet is $5, your larger bet would be $20, up to $135 of winnings. Winnings of $200 would mean the larger bet would be $30; $300 ahead would mean a larger bet of $45, and so on.

An aggressive formula for the same size stake would be a base bet of $10, with a ratio of 1 to 4, and the larger

Figure 8

RATIOS AND BASE BETS FOR WINNING SITUATIONS

	STAKE	% OF WINNINGS TO RAISE HIGHER BET OF RATIO	MINIMUM RATIO WHEN AHEAD	BASE BET
CONSERVATIVE	$ 300	15%	1 to 3	$ 5
	500	15	1 to 4	5
	1,000	20	1 to 4	15
	2,500	20	1 to 4	25
AGGRESSIVE	$ 300	20%	1 to 4	5
	500	20	1 to 4	10
	1,000	25	1 to 5	25
	2,500	25	1 to 5	50

bet raised 20 percent of your winnings. In this case the ratio would not be raised until your winnings were more than $200. Since a $10 base bet would mean a larger bet of $40 when using a 1 to 4 ratio, this takes in all winnings up to, and including, $200. Winnings of $300 would mean a larger bet of $60; $400 ahead would mean a larger bet of $80, and so on.

Figure 7, in the previous chapter, outlined starting ratios, and should be followed fairly closely to prevent rapid losses and bets out of proportion to your bankroll. Figure 8 differs from Figure 7 in that it is to be used only when winning, and is merely a guide. When you are playing with the casino's money you should have a bit more leeway and can afford more of a risk.

When bets are raised, certain rules must be followed:

• 1. Should you fall below the winnings at which point you

raised the base bet or ratio, immediately revert back to the previous bet.

- 2. Always revert back to the original base bet and ratio if you fall back to your original stake, or start losing.
- 3. Raise the higher ratio bet before raising the smaller base bet.

The third rule is probably the most difficult for a winner to follow. Rule three, however, is the very basis of this sytem of gaining a percentage over the house. It does not imply that a player with a few thousand dollars in front of him should remain with a $25 base bet. It is the spread between the two bets, though, that gains the percentages for the player.

The base bet may seem small in comparison to the larger ratio bet, but this smaller bet is placed on an average of 68 percent of the time; the other 32 percent of the bets being the larger ones. This can be a considerable amount if the player that started with $1,000 should be fortunate enough to run $600 ahead. If playing a 1 to 6 ratio, and a base bet as low as $25, the second bet would be $150, split or doubled to $300. This amount exceeds a prudent bet for the knowledgeable player.

As outlined in the chapters on the win-loss group system, the larger ratio bets are placed at propitious instances throughout the game, and are calculated to pay off at a higher rate than the smaller bets. Taking the blackjack bonus and the gains from splits and doubles into consideration, consider the following:

The 32 percent of the time that you place the second bet of the ratio—no matter what proportion it is to the base bet—your winnings (not hands played) will exceed your losses by 4 percent. The 68 percent of the time that you place the first bet of the ratio, your *losses will exceed your winnings* by 4 percent. In other words, keep the first ratio (base) bet as low as practical.

One of the few players employing this system (prior to the completion of this book), started playing with a stake of $300. Over a few hours of play, she possessed the fortitude to remain with a $5 base bet (despite the looks of other players at the table that implied she had foolishly lost money by not knowing how to increase bets), and walked away from the table with a total of $1,175. The top bet placed (the second ratio bet) was $80, at a point that she was $800 ahead. She increased the second bet 10 percent of her winnings, to a high ratio of 1 to 16.

Admittedly, this is not the average amount of winnings for this size stake. But if averaged, however, with smaller amounts of winnings and the times that the $300 may have been partially, or completely, lost, it would show this player on the plus side very close to a proportion of her average percentage gain of the ratios used throughout her playing sessions.

The formula she used is extremely conservative. Although highly recommended, there are those of you that look for a little faster action. Though I firmly advise not to try for a large percentage gain at the beginning of play, try the aggressive formulas outlined in Figures 7 and 8.

The proper bets, combined with a good basic strategy, form a winning combination. Though we all play to win, avarice and greed will take your money much faster than the casinos will take your money.

CHAPTER 15

When to Stop

When to end a particular visit to a casino is one of the many facets of money management that too often causes a player to grumble, "I should have quit while I was ahead." Leaving the table while ahead should be given careful thought prior to sitting down to play. What are your goals? Small winnings? Going for broke? Winning a percentage of your stake? Many factors will probably influence your decision, such as how often you visit a casino, distance travelled, expenses involved, and perhaps most important, your own personal finances. Whatever the reasons, decide on a realistic objective and firmly stick to it.

The mounts that you wager should depend on the size of your stake and, during the game, whether you are ahead or behind. How much is won or lost during a particular session, therefore, depends on the starting stake. The results of a session started with $500 would not be the same as if that same session were started with $2,000.

This fact must be taken into consideration when determining at what point to leave the table if winning. If starting with $100, it is just as unrealistic to set a goal of $1,000 in winnings as it is to start with $1000 and have $100 as the goal.

We previously discussed how to try to recoup losses—and that was by minimum bets and a good deal of patience. Winning must be treated a bit differently, as we are not trying to reverse a trend, as while losing.

If you ended the session each time that you found yourself the slightest amount ahead, you would probably win more often than you would lose—for the majority of the time you will usually find yourself, at one point or another, ahead. Unfortunately, winning more often than losing does not necessarily keep you ahead of the game.

If you start with $300 and are prepared (though not willingly) to lose the entire amount, the method of quitting with small winnings may allow you to boast of more winning than losing sessions. You will, however, fall behind in dollars. The small amounts won would not make up for the times that the $300 may be entirely lost. If your intentions are (if losing), to stop at a point less than a $300 loss, then the $300 cannot be considered your original stake.

If, on the other hand, you just played on forever, the wins and losses would balance out to the average percentage that you are playing ahead of, or behind, the house. This method may well cause you to be the one to complain about not quitting while ahead.

Using the $300 stake as an example, the following suggestions are offered:

• Decide on a percentage of your stake that would be a

minimum amount with which to leave the table. A logical amount would be about 30 percent, rounded out to $100 (with the $300 stake).

- To this amount add increments of $50 (50 percent).
- If you go over the $100 minimum goal, do not stop playing, as further winnings may be in store. Keep going until you reach either $150 or fall back to $100. Falling back should be the end of this session and a fulfillment of your original goal.

Going ahead, however, would set up a new minimum amount of $150 to fall back to before leaving the table, and at the same time a new plateau of $200 would be the next goal. If winnings continue, keep raising both minimum and maximum goals. Remember to keep raising the higher bet of the ratio being played.

It is simple enough to proportion your own bankroll to the amounts used in the above example. The minimum goal with a $1,000 stake would be $300 with increments of $150, which are the same percentages as in the $300 example, and so on.

If you have been doing a bit of playing, I am certain that you can recall many occasions that this method would have allowed you to go home a winner, rather than with memories of winnings that were returned to the casino.

> *True luck consists not in holding the best of cards at the table;*
> *Luckiest is he who knows just when to rise and go home.*
>
> —John Hay

CHAPTER 16

Potpourri

Some players make so many bad moves that they remind me of "the curious horse," to wit:

"Did you win at the track today?" asked the wife.

"No," said the disgusted husband. "I think my horse just ran out of curiosity."

"Out of curiosity?"

"Yeah, he just wanted to see if other horses also have fannies."

I have spoken to hundreds of players to gain an insight into their reasons for playing a particular type of game. I felt that information gained by discussing their actions would be an asset to this book and of interest to all players. At no time did I start a conversation while a game was in progress, but when I observed interesting plays that were in opposition to a recommended basic strategy, and the player seemed amenable, I would pose a question during the time that the cards were being shuffled or when the player left the

table. I was never refused an explanation for the plays that
I had witnessed, nor did I try to offer advice if I thought
the plays were bad. Most players were eager to defend
their moves with theories that, on the surface, appeared logical, but theory and counter-theory should be of interest to
all.

Scared Money Never Wins

I spent about an hour watching one of two players at
a $100 minimum-bet table. This player had three to four
thousand dollars in $100 denomination chips, and all his
bets were either $100 or $200, with no noticeable system
as to why he varied the amount.

He signalled moves quickly and decisively, and followed a good basic strategy, which led me to believe that
he knew the game well. Unfortunately though, things were
going badly and his pile of chips kept decreasing steadily. I
noticed at this time, that he would hesitate before making
a decision when his hand totalled a 15 or 16 and a hit was
called for. The more he lost, the more he hesitated on these
two hands, and despite knowing that to hit was the proper
move—for he had been hitting previously—he would stand.
This player had fallen into the trap of knowing that
his chances of breaking were more than 50 percent when
his hand totalled 15 or 16, despite the fact that he knew
these totals should be hit against a dealer's up-cards of 7 to
ace.

I was truly sorry to see him leave the table, at the end
of about one hour, with no chips remaining. The look on
his face discouraged me from asking why he made these
moves against, what I would bet on, was his better judge-

ment. I would venture a guess though, that the more he lost, the more he became fearful of breaking, despite his knowledge of the percentages.

If You Don't Break You're Still in the Game

This syndrome seems to affect players desperately trying to hold on to money, and results in overruling good judgement.

I have had this one thrown at me a number of times. In each case the player theorized that the greatest drawback to the blackjack player was that if he broke, the game was lost whether the dealer did or did not break, and the perfect counter-play was never to break.

This "drawback" theory is correct; the counter-play is not. The player that does not hit a stiff hand (12 to 16 total) to a dealer's up-card of a 7 to an ace, loses over 75 percent more of the losses incurred on these card combinations than the player that hits them. Conversely, the player that will hit these combinations will not always break—but correctly played—will break on an average of about 55 percent of the time.

If It's Good Enough for the Dealer, It's Good Enough for Me.

In contrast to the "never break" theory, this expression and method of play is evidently not too popular, as I have heard this expression only once, and witnessed players following this theory no more than three times.

No splits or double downs; no standing on stiff hands. I had no occasion to question any of these players, but after about 10 minutes of watching one player—who hit, rather than split aces—the player to his left did ask, "How come?" The reply he received was, "If it's good enough for the dealer, it's good enough for me."

Sure enough, he won that hand, and turning to the player that questioned him, smugly said, "See what I mean?"

This player actually believed that the house made its percentages by the rules governing the dealer's action, completely oblivious to the overwhelming edge the house picks up by the "mutual break" rule, where the house wins the hand. He thought that he could even out the odds by mimicking the dealer, disregarding the fact that if he broke with a total of 25 and the dealer broke with a total of 22, he beat the dealer—but lost the bet.

Burned Cards

"Why does a new dealer always have to burn the top card when taking over?" a player once complained to me. "Its nonsense! No need for it. If I'm doing OK when he comes in and burns the card, I usually stay out for one hand to bring the cards back in order."

No comment.

I Haven't Had a Blackjack in an Hour

Although the time limit may vary, this complaint would probably head the list of "remarks most often heard."

If a player could keep track of blackjacks and the number of hands played, he would be amazed to find how close to 4.74 percent of the time that he was being dealt a blackjack. After just a few hours of play the blackjacks would average out to within 1 percent of this figure, and a running count over a period of time would soon narrow down to within .2 percent.

I Double Any Two Cards Against a Dealer's 5 or 6

I had watched this player double down on a total of 5 against a dealer's up-card of 5. This move left no chance of reaching a total of 17 or over, which would, at the very least, give him the chance of a push if the dealer did not break.

His reasoning was that the dealer could easily break if showing a 5. The fact is that he will break only about 44 percent of the time, taking this player's double bet the other 56 percent.

I Always Break When I Hit a 16

Not true. *Most* of the time—about 61 percent—but not always. But even with this large percentage of breaks, the player will lose less by hitting a 16 against a dealer's 7, 8, 9, 10, or ace.

I Never Split 9's Because 18 is Such a Good Hand

This player is losing an overall average of .25 percent.

I Usually Hit a 16, but Never Against a 7

"Why?" I asked. No answer. "Is it because 16 is so close to 17?" An affirmative shrug.

The fact is that hitting a 16 to a dealer's 7 will produce more winning hands than hitting a 16 to a dealer's 8, 9, 10, or ace.

I Win Most of the Time When I Split 10's

Contrary to the popular notion that a hand should not be hit if it breaks or loses the majority of the time, is the tendency to make certain moves that win most of the time, e.g., splitting 10's.

Hitting a 10 *will* result in winning over 50 percent of the time, but if the 10 is the result of splitting a two-card total of 20, you will take a loss of 37 percent on this move, and an overall loss of 3.5 percent.

Most players that make this play do so against a dealer's up-card of a 2 to a 6. But even against a 6 (an up-card that seems to make players forget they ever heard of a basic strategy), and the tremendous probability of winning 62 percent of the time, you will take a loss of 14 percent on this move, and an overall loss of 1.3 percent.

Lady Luck at Her Finest

During my many hours of blackjack "watching," I spent about one hour observing a young fellow who, aside from the fact that he had a few too many, was playing one of the worst games that I had witnessed. His plays were so bad that the dealer constantly questioned his choices. Some typical plays were: standing on a soft 15, hitting a total of 14 to a dealer's up-card of 6, and standing on a 12 to a dealer's 10.

This player was sitting in the seventh seat, and during this period of time I saw two players leave the table in disgust, after mouthing disparaging remarks (both their exits and remarks were, in my opinion, uncalled for). He was betting from one to five red ($5) chips per hand, and by the end of an hour had increased his stake by about $200. By pure mental guesswork, I calculated that he must have been playing 10 to 20 percent behind the house. Simple luck when placing his larger bets was what put him ahead.

At the risk of sounding redundant, I must once again repeat my warning concerning "averaging out over an extended period of play." I have no doubt that if he were to always play this way, and it wasn't the result of the vast amount of beer that he kept consuming, he had previously suffered many serious losses, and that his (temporary) winning would not last.

This just proves the volatile nature of the game of blackjack. As easily as this player had won $200, the most accomplished blackjack player in the world could lose a like amount.

Change Please

I saw a woman dash over to a table and drop two green ($25) chips into the betting circle of the third position. Within one second the dealer dealt the first card, at which time the woman said, ". . . wait, I want change." The dealer turned to the pit boss, but they had no option except to inform her that she had placed a $50 bet, and at that point it was irrevocable. She lost the bet and immediately left the table. I couldn't quite determine if she felt faint or was broke.

Never place any chips into the betting circle (or square) that is not a wager.

Enough material to fill another book can be gathered by observing and talking to blackjack players. The point to keep in mind is that plays made with no knowledge of, or contrary to, a good basic strategy, will lose percentages for the player, causing winnings to be smaller and losses greater.

The real name of the game is not blackjack, roulette, craps, baccarat, or any other casino game, but rather "Beat the House," and knowing the odds, my friend, is the only way that you have a prayer of a chance.

> *For most men (till by losing rendered sager)*
> *Will back their own opinions by a wager.*

—Lord Byron

Appendix

The percentages outlined in Figure 9 show how multiple decks slow up the probabilities that are the backbone of all card-counting systems. To simplify the example, we will assume that we are seeking a card other than a 10, although proportionally it does not matter.

The percentage probability of a 2 appearing on the first turn of a card from either one or eight decks is identical. Assuming that the 2 does not turn up, we can see the dramatic increase in the probabilities of it appearing in the one-deck play—as opposed to the slower probabilities in the eight-deck play—as the card is sought up to the following 30 cards. It is this increase in probabilities that the card-counter can turn to his advantage in anticipating percentages of possible wins or losses.

Comparison of these figures graphically demonstrates how playing against eight decks, as compared to one deck,

Figure 9

PERCENTAGE DIFFERENCES BETWEEN PLAYING
AGAINST ONE DECK AND EIGHT DECKS

	1 DECK		8 DECKS	
	% CHANCE OF TURNING A 2	% INCREASE FROM 1st TURN	% CHANCE OF TURNING A 2	% INCREASE FROM 1st TURN
1st CARD	7.69		7.69	
2nd CARD	7.84	1.95	7.71	.26
5th CARD	8.51	10.66	7.79	1.30
10th CARD	9.52	23.80	7.88	2.47
30th CARD	18.18	136.42	8.29	7.80

diminishes card-counting capabilities. Though the first card in each case had a 7.69 percent probability of turning up as a 2, by the time the 30th card was reached, the chances of the 2 appearing had increased to 18.18 percent in the one-deck deal and to only 8.29 percent in the eight-deck deal. This was a 136.42 percent increase in the first instance, but only a 7.8 percent increase in the other.

With only 30 cards played, which could very well be only the second round of hands played, the one-deck probabilities advanced 17.49 times further than the eight-deck probabilities. It is not hard to see how the casinos put a dent into card-counting techniques by utilizing multiple decks.

On the other hand, as the non-counter must consider each shoe to be neutral, which it is when averaged throughout the playing of the shoe, the only disadvantage to the player is the lower number of blackjacks that may be expected. This is reduced from 4.82 percent to 4.74 percent. Not exactly desirable when we strive to gain each fraction of a percent, but a change with which we can live.

Drawing to a 12 Against One Deck and Eight Decks

A change that will be quickly noticed by the experienced blackjack player between the strategy recommended in this book and any other strategy that may be used by the player, is to stand on a total of 12 to a dealer's up-card of a 2. For our example we will use a 12 consisting of a 10 and 2—the most common combination of this total.

The percentages noted in the columns headed "draw"

are the results of drawing only one card, for if the player reached a total of 13 to 16, he would stand against a dealer's 2.

Figure 10

RESULTS AGAINST A ONE-DECK GAME

	DRAW	STAND
PUSH	05.01%	00.00%
LOSE	56.95	61.31
WIN	38.04	38.69
TOTAL LOSS	18.91%	22.62%

One can readily see that, although both plays will average out to losses, there is a definite advantage to be gained—a 16.4 percent smaller loss—by drawing a card.

In an eight-deck game the results are quite different. With the same hand of a 10 and a 2 facing a dealer's up-card of 2, we now see the following:

Figure 11

RESULTS AGAINST AN EIGHT-DECK GAME

	DRAW	STAND
PUSH	04.60%	00.00%
LOSE	57.85	59.26
WIN	37.55	40.74
TOTAL LOSS	20.30%	18.52%

Once again we see losses either way, but in this case if the player were to draw a card he would take a 9·6 percent *additional* loss on this move.

Win-Loss Groups per 100 Hands

The possibility of having from one to 50 individual groups per 100 tosses is theoretically possible, but extreme deviations from the total groups of the 25 noted in Figure 5 is extremely rare. One (1) group would mean that either all 100 tosses were either heads or tails, while 50 groups would be the result of no two heads or tails falling consecutively, e.g., the tosses would have to fall head, tail, head, tail, etc.

The probability of either of these two events occurring is one in many trillions. The odds narrow progressively as the number of groups approach the average.

Playing the basic strategy as outlined in this book, 150 random samples—each containing 100 hands of blackjack (for a total of 15,000 individual hands)—produced the following results:*

Average number of individual groups of consecutive wins or losses	24.7
Percentage of groups below 12 percent of average...	70%
Percentage of groups at 12 percent of average	15%
Percentage of groups at 16 percent of average	9%
Percentage of groups at 20 percent of average	4%
Percentage of groups at 24 percent of average	2%
Percentage of groups over 24 percent of average...	0

*The total number of hands were all winning or losing hands, disregarding pushes. If two wins were recorded followed by a push and another win, it was regarded as three consecutive winning hands.

These figures demonstrate that although possibilities (not probabilities) may range from one to 50 groups of wins or losses per 100 hands, actual play produced a range of from a low of 19 groups to a high of 31 groups. And even these two extremes (which are not even close to the possibility of one to 50 groups) appeared only 2 percent of the time, or three times throughout the 150 samples.

Chance; noun. The unknown or the undefined cause of events not subject to calculation; luck; fortune.

—Britannica Edition of Funk & Wagnall's Standard Dictionary

* * *

Chance favors the prepared mind.

—Louis Pasteur

Work and acquire, and thou has chained the wheel of *chance*.

—R. W. Emerson

Nothing comes by *chance*, for, in all the wide universe there is absolutely no such thing as *chance*. We bring whatever comes. Are we not satisfied with effects, the results? The thing to do is to change the causes.

—R. W. Trine

* * *

Funk and Wagnall; or Pasteur, Emerson, and Trine?